J
796.8
Wa

Ward, Don
Andre, the giant

ALL-STAR WRESTLING
ANDRE THE GIANT

PHOTOGRAPHIC CREDITS

WIDE WORLD PHOTO: ALL PHOTOS

Published by Creative Education, Inc., 123 South Broad Street, Mankato, Minnesota 56001

Library of Congress Catalog Card No.: 86-72532

ISBN 0-88682-089-8

ALL-STAR WRESTLING
ANDRE THE GIANT
BY DON WARD

CREATIVE EDUCATION

The Giant Brought Tears To Japan . . . Ooomph! The Japanese will remember 1986 as the year their mightiest grappler—Antonio Inoki—finally got pinned.

Inoki is the same guy who had squared off against Muhammad Ali in a weird wrestling/boxing match several years earlier. "No one pins Inoki," boasted a Japanese promoter as his hero stepped into the ring against the Giant. No one beats Andre, either. Someone had to give. It was Inoki losing by a Giant Pin.

Tears flowed freely at ringside that night. As for Andre, he just smiled and bid Sayonara to the heartbroken fans.

"It was the most stunning event in Japanese wrestling history," said a Japanese promoter who was quoted in the Wrestling Tattler. "One minute, the crowd is going crazy, chanting all kinds of things and urging on the wrestlers. Then, before anybody knew it, Andre pins Inoki and this incredible hush comes over the crowd.

"Imagine, the great Inoki getting pinned! It's

simply unheard-of in this country. Even Andre seemed to be unsure of what he had done."

☆ ☆ ☆

Lonely Giant ... Inside the ring, Andre is slow to anger, but ferocious when finally aroused.

Outside the ring, however, the Giant is very quiet, almost tender. At home in Grenoble, France, he is known as a gentle, solitary man who enjoys a stroll through the park or a lazy afternoon at the beach.

Unlike some of the other big-name wrestlers, Andre is never rowdy or gruff in public. A neighbor once described him as "a peaceful, loving man who wants to be friends with everyone. Unfortunately, the Giant has trouble meeting new people because of his size and appearance. I once saw Andre try to strike up a conversation with a lady at a bakery—and she fainted."

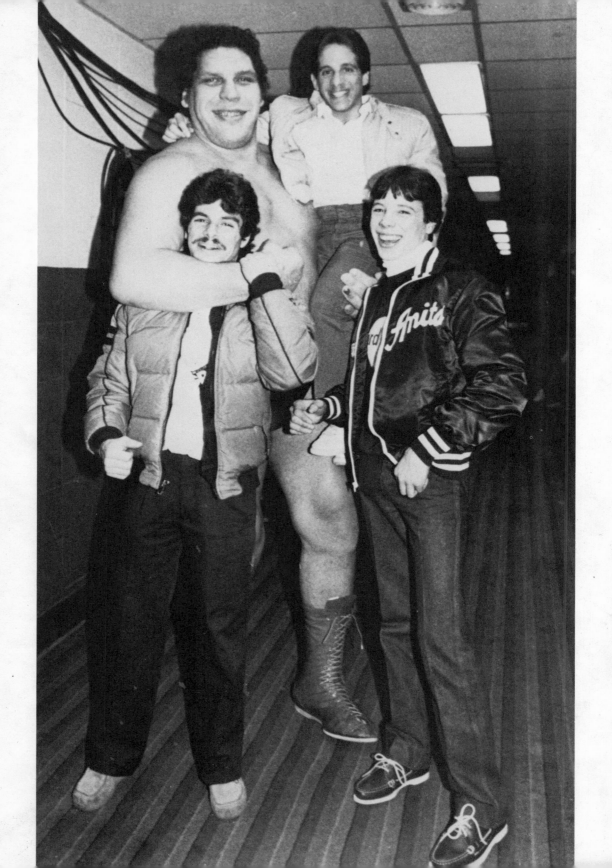

On another occasion, an elderly woman saw Andre at a bus stop. After watching him carefully for a few minutes, the woman walked up behind the Giant and poked him with her umbrella.

"I just wanted to see if you were real," she said when Andre turned around. Andre smiled courteously, of course, but there was a sad expression in his eyes. It's lonely being a giant.

☆ ☆ ☆

No More Killer Kahn ... Many of the very biggest men in wrestling have also been among the slowest and the most fragile. Andre, however, is not only cat-quick—he's durable. Only once in his entire career has he sustained a serious injury.

"The injury occurred during a match with Killer Kahn in Boston," recounts George Napolitano in Wrestling Heroes and Villains. "Kahn knocked Andre to the mat. The Mongolion mounted the ring ropes and then came crashing down from the third rope, breaking Andre's leg in two places.

"Andre spent the next two weeks in the hospital and then had to hobble around on crutches for two more weeks. You just had to know that someday Andre would get his sweet revenge on Kahn—and he did. After Andre got through with Kahn, the Mongolian madman took the next plane headed to 'Outer Mongolia' and never returned to the World Wrestling Federation."

★ ★ ★

An Unscheduled Haircut ... According to legend, Sampson's strength was in his hair.

"Maybe Andre's strength is in that bushy black mop on his big ugly head, too," said Big John Studd, the Giant's archrival. It was then that Studd got together with Bobby Heenan and Ken Patera. The three ganged up on Andre in the ring one night, knocked him senseless and cut off his hair with an enormous pair of pinking sheers.

For weeks, Andre steamed as Patera, Studd and Heenan ran around crowing to reporters about

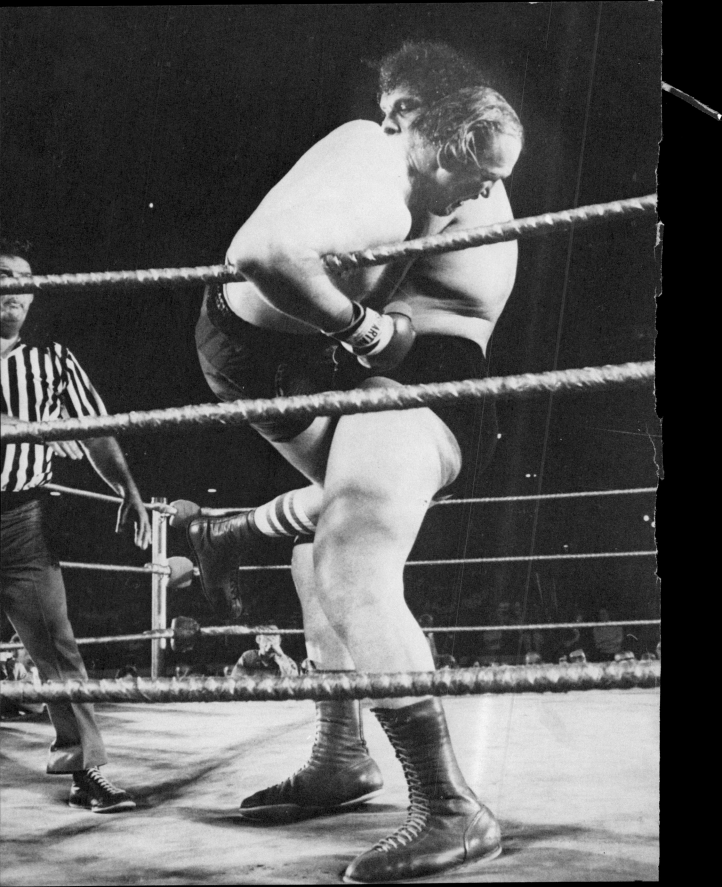

their accomplishment. They could run, but they couldn't hide. Andre finally caught up to Patera at WrestleMania and—you guessed it. The body-slam! At last report, Studd and Heenan were still running . . . but this time, very quietly!

☆ ☆ ☆

His One Fear . . . A curious reporter at Wrestle-Mania asked Andre an unusual question: "What does a 500-pound man fear the most?"

Andre thought for a moment before softly replying, "There is no man on earth who frightens me in combat, but I admit that I am scared of one thing. Everyone is scared of the future, of the unknown. I know that the day will come when I must step out of the ring forever. When that will be, I don't really know. But, when it comes, I must be prepared.

"Wrestling has been so good to me. It has allowed me to travel the world, make friends and meet people everywhere. Will there be a good life for me when my wrestling days are over? I don't know. I can only hope."

☆ ☆ ☆

King Of The Ring ... What happens when you toss a dozen men in the ring for a free-for-all with the Giant? That's exactly what happened at WrestleMania II in Chicago. The awestruck editors of the August, 1986 Wrestling Bulletin reported the mayhem this way:

"Andre The Giant, who stands 7-foot-4 and claims to weigh more than 500 pounds was the last man in the ring in the Battle Royale at Rosemont Horizon in Suburban Chicago.

"He won this 'King of the Ring' against thirteen other wrestlers and National League Football players, including William Perry (The Chicago Bears' famed Refrigerator) Jim Covert, Bill Fralic, Harvey Martin and Russ Francis.

"Of the NFL'ers, Francis was the last to go over the ropes. Perry finished a respectable sixth, after

16

being eliminated by Big John Studd. Perry retaliated by pulling out Studd, and the team of Jim "The Anvil" Neidhart and Brett "Hitman" Hart.

As for the Giant, he stood alone in the ring at the end—unhurt, unbowed and unbeaten as always.

☆ ☆ ☆

Showdown With The Hulk ... As this book went to press, the rumor from Japan was that Andre was pulling out of all further matches and going into secret, Tokyo-based training sessions in preparation for a single dream title match with the great Hulk Hogan.

Hogan, the WWF world champion, is the best-loved wrestler of all time, or so the polls say. He is also in the prime of his career. Andre, of course, is a fan favorite, too. But time is running out on his career.

"I am no longer a young man by wrestling standards," admitted Andre in a recent Japanese newspaper article. "I must meet Hogan now, not later. I will defeat him, just as I have defeated every other man who has tested me. Beware, Mr. Hogan—the old giant has one more victory inside him."

Sadly, however, most wrestling experts doubt that Andre will ever get his chance to meet Hogan for the belt. You see, the World Wrestling Federation never pits two fan favorites against each other, preferring instead to feature a good guy like Hulk against a despicable rule-breaker like King Kong Bundy. Ironically, Andre may miss his last shot at the title simply because he's a nice guy who wrestles cleanly and honestly by the rules.

By the way, the Hulk and the Giant actually faced each other back in 1980 when Hogan wrestled as a rulebreaker under the management of Fred Blassie.

"Andre scored a pinfall," recounts the Fall, 1986 edition of Wrestling SuperStars, "but tapes of the match indicate that Hogan managed to kick out

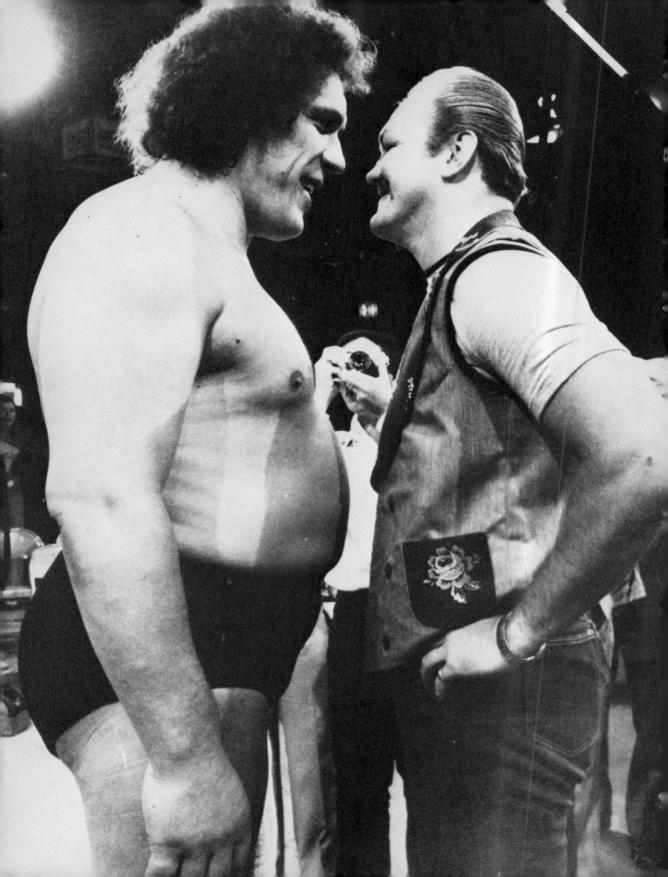

just before the referee completed the three-count. After the match, Blassie placed an object in Hogan's elbowpad, and The Hulkster proceeded to mercilessly bloody the Giant."

☆ ☆ ☆

Battle Of The Giants ... From Wrestling World Mag comes this eyewitness account of the spectacular 1986 King Kong Bundy versus Andre The Giant bout at Fresno's Convention Center. What made this match-up a doozie—what made it something that electrified the 9,000 fans that evening—was the fact that here at last were the two biggest men in all of wrestling together at last in the same ring:

"The final event of the evening was billed as the 'Battle of the Giants.' The Eighth Wonder of the World, Andre the Giant, standing 7-foot-4 and weighing 484 pounds, took on King Kong Bundy, a 453-pounder from Atlantic City.

"Bundy forced Andre to his knees and for several moments he held the Giant in a reverse wristlock, but the big man refused to give up. Bundy lost his temper and attempted to smother Andre.

"Finally the massive Frenchman climbed to his feet, picked Bundy up, and dropped him, as the fans laughed it up. Two minutes later, Andre tripped Bundy and held him in a reverse cradle for the three-count. To say that Bundy was upset would be putting it mildly.

"'I'll get even with that bum,' he screamed. 'His size doesn't frighten me. I'm the second-biggest man in wrestling, and as soon as I get rid of him, I'll be the biggest.'"

☆ ☆ ☆

It's The Fat Farm For Andre ... "If you ask me," wrote a fan in a recent issue of Inside Wrestling, "the WWF shouldn't stand for World Wrestling Federation, it should stand for 'where wrestlers fatten up.'

"I can't believe what's happened to so many of my favorite wrestlers over the years. Magnificent Muraco, once an agile athlete and perhaps the most dangerous man anywhere in wrestling, has become an overblown and puffy caricature of what he once was.

"Adrian Adonis, a man who never was in fantastic shape, used to have a body that was at least firm; now, Adonis' barrel chest makes him look ridiculous, and the waves of fat that wash over his stomach prevent me from taking him seriously as a wrestler anymore.

"Andre the Giant, while never a poster boy for Jack LaLanne, has developed a belly that threatens to touch his toes—something I'm sure Andre hasn't done in years."

NOTE: Andre himself admits that he has let himself go completely in recent years, but blames the WWF for failing to come up with any opponents who can give him a decent tussle. As mentioned elsewhere in this book, however, Andre has recently gone into serious training in the hopes of earning a title shot against one wrestler who keeps himself in supreme physical condition—the great Hulk Hogan.

☆ ☆ ☆

What The Experts Say About The Possible Dream Match Between Andre The Giant And The Hulk . . .

"Andre vs. Hulk would be like WW-III," says promoter Frankie Liewelyn. "I really can't envision either man giving in until all the nukes have been wheeled out, launched and exploded."

"A mind-boggling possibility," says referee Mike Dbyszko. "I would give anything to officiate such a match. There wouldn't be an empty seat in the house, the whole sports world would flood the closed-circuit houses, and for good reason. It would be history in the making."

"My mother despises wrestling," says WWF spokesman Cory Lambright, "but even she would want a frontrow seat to this match. Figure it out.

Here's The Giant who is undefeated in his entire career but never a champion. Here's The Hulk who is the all-time greatest celebrity in wrestling history. We owe so much to both men—the fans would have a fit figuring out who to root for.

"Personally, I'd like to see The Giant win and then immediately retire at the top."